738.140^D 63947.

VAN, Gerda Wijmans see...

Ceramic techniques

Ceramic techniques

van Dobbenburgh Amsterdam/Kidderminster

438.14

Original titel. Keramische technieken
Editor: Gerda Wijmans van Dillen
Translation from the Dutch
The Old Rectory, Pyworthy,
Holsworthy, Devon. Ex 22 6LA, England

English Edition distributed by
Ruskin Book services Ltd.
15 Comberton Hill, Kidderminster
Worcestershire DY 10 1QG U.K.
Telephone 0562 515151 and 68014
Telex RBS 335672
Printed in Spain by I.G. Domingo, S.A. San Joan Despí

ISBN 9-06-577031-3

Contents

Introduction

This book forms a step-by-step guide to the creation of ceramic works with the help of many useful illustrations. A number of simple exercises have been chosen as an initial stimulus to practise the skills involved.
It discusses the Typeface of *tools* needed to work in the medium.
The book can be used by individuals or for work in groups.
It deals in detail with technical problems such as wedging, working with a wheel, repetition throwing, modelling, glazing and firing. The projects described do not appear in an arbitrary order but are based on the skill which must be learned for each section.
Apart from this, each subject is dealt with separately.
The chapter on glazing describes a number of essential basic concepts.
This illustrated course contains enough information for the beginner to acquire the necessary technical skills.
When he has gained enough experience he will then find it possible and desirable to determine the form and content of his own works.

Clay and tools

Ceramic ware is the collective term for all objects which are made of clay. The word derives from the Greek 'keramikè', which means 'the potter's art'.
Clay is available almost everywhere and its usefulness was discovered by man at the dawn of history. It might even be claimed that pottery is one of the oldest crafts. Over the centuries potters have developed as artists. In the past the craft was passed on from father to son and the secrets of the composition of the clay or the ingredients of the glazes were carefully guarded. As a result of industrialization pots were no longer made by hand as this had become far too expensive, but it is quite remarkable how many people nowadays feel the need to take up pottery. Clay is easily available and there are courses where you can learn how to make pots, as well as the many books on the subject. In fact, pottery is becoming an increasingly popular leisure activity. This book deals with the most essential procedures step-by-step. When you have read it, you won't be a perfect potter, but you'll certainly be on the way to mastering the art.

You can order different qualities of clay in virtually any shop selling artists' materials. It is usually sold by the kilogram or sometimes in 'loaves' of ten and twenty-five kilograms. It is also a good idea to buy the following tools and pieces of equipment.

1. various modelling tools (a good shop will be happy to advise on this);
2. a sponge – if possible, a genuine one;
3. modelling spatulas;
4. good brushes (cheap brushes lose their bristles and this can cause problems);
5. a clay cutter (two wooden rods attached to approximately 45 cm of twisted stainless steel wire);
6. plasterboard;
7. a rolling pin.

The wheel

Using the wheel is not as easy as it looks.
Nearly everyone has seen a potter at his wheel at one time or another, but the ease with which he conjures up objects from the clay is very misleading. It requires many years of practice. According to Japanese potters, a lifetime is not long enough to turn a single flawless pot. The potter's wheel was used at least 7,000 years ago in Egypt and was one of the first pieces of sophisticated machinery to be used by man.
A great deal of patience and perseverance is required to learn to master this important aspect to the potter's art. There are various different types of wheel and two of them are shown here.

A. The kick wheel, which is put into motion with the foot on the bottom wheel and continues turning under its own weight.

B. The electric wheel is most widely used because it takes up less space and requires less effort.
The speed is regulated by means of a lever or pedal. There are many different types of electric wheels, but all are more expensive – both to buy and to use – than a kick wheel.

Different types of clay and their characteristics

A plastic bag full of pennies and a little bit of water can be pushed into all sorts of shapes. When the water is removed by pricking holes in the plastic and the bag is again tied up, the volume is smaller and it becomes less malleable.

When the water in a lump of clay evaporates, the volume decreases in the same way and the clay becomes less easy to work. Clay shrinks when it dries out. The comparison with a plastic bag full of pennies is not really so strange, because in a damp lump of clay the flat particles slide over one another, surrounded by water. When the water evaporates, these particles stick together. When they are greasy they slide easily one over the other. A distinction can be made between oily and thin clay, or between plastic and non-plastic clay. Clay which is found in the place where it was formed as a result of the erosion of rocks containing feldspar is not plastic clay. Clay which is found a long way away from the place where its was formed, carried there by rivers or glaciers, has a finer structure and is therefore more plastic.

To make the clay less oily, non-plastic materials are added such as quartz or sand, as well as 'grog' (clay which has been fired and has then been ground fine). If you want to increase the plasticity of the clay bentonite can be added. This type of clay is described under illustration 7 of this chapter. Clay which contains iron turns a pink or red colour when it is fired, depending on the percentage of iron oxide. The glaze which is chosen and its firing temperature determine which type of clay is to be used. Its structure should be such that the glaze will stick to it; the structure must not be too fragile when the firing temperature of the glaze is reached.

Clay for stoneware which is fired at 1200° C. cannot be glazed with a glaze which has a firing temperature of 900° C; the glaze will not usually adhere satisfactorily.

1. Brick clay. This contains many impurities. When it is fired it will be a yellowish or reddish colour depending on the content of iron oxides. It is used for household articles (jugs, pots, etc.) Firing temperature: 850 - 1000° C.

2. Potter's clay. Also known as red clay. It is used a great deal by potters and for modelling. After firing it is a deep red or brown colour. Firing temperature: 900 - 1050° C. At higher temperatures it will be deformed. It has a high plasticity.

3. Stoneware clay. This clay contains sufficient feldspar to act as a melting agent, so that it becomes vitreous at 1300° C. When it has been fired it is extremely plastic and non-absorbent with a greyish or creamy colour.

4. 'Ball clay'. English clay. This clay is a grey or black colour because of the high content of organic matter, but after firing it goes white. It is a very oily clay which is not used on its own because it shrinks considerably. However, it is added to clay used for art pottery and porcelain to produce something with greater plasticity, which is more durable and less transparent.

5. Kaolin. Also known as 'porcelain clay'. This is the purest clay available. The shard or fired material of washed kaolin is virtually pure white.
It is not very plastic and is extremely heat resistant. It is never used on its own, but is usually mixed with other types of clay (for example, ball clay). Because of its white colour it is eminently suitable for porcelain. The firing temperature is 1250° C. for soft, 1450° C. for hard porcelain.

6. Fire clay. This is very heat resistant clay with a melting point of about 1500°C. For this reason it is used for the manufacture of oven bricks and to form wall mouldings. Depending on the content and type of impurities in this clay, different interesting textures can be achieved. For wall mouldings (fired and ground clay of the same type) is added.

7. Bentonite. A type of clay with volcanic origins. It has extremely plastic qualities because the particles are extremely fine. There are two sorts of bentonite, one of which can hold four or five times its own volume of water. It can be added to clay used to make art pottery or porcelain. However, there should not be more than 3% of bentonite as cracks will otherwise form in the products. This is because bentonite has a high iron content and consequently shrinks a great deal.

Kneading qualities and consistency of clay

To work with clay it must have a certain degree of plasticity which can usually be easily obtained by adding water, though you must be careful not to add too much water. When the water has been added, lie the clay on a plaster board which in turn removes excess water. The clay will also dry out through being in contact with air. Sometimes water alone is not sufficient and other materials have to be added, for example, the plastic type of clay, bentonite. Of course, there are other ways of making the clay more pliable, for example, by exposing it to bacteria in the open air. An old method used in the past was to urinate all over it. The Ancient Chinese would leave the clay to rot in water for decades. There were 'clay testers' in the tiling factories on the banks of the wide rivers.

1

Dry clay – unusable without adding water.

2

Water is added to obtain the plasticity needed for clay modelling or potting. Leave the water to soak in.

They were able to tell whether the clay was ready to use by tasting it. In its dry form, clay still contains water (so-called 'crystal water' or chemically bound water). This is built into the molecules. A molecule of any material is the smallest particle which still contains the characteristics of that material. The more water the plate-shaped molecules contain, the greater the plasticity of the clay. When the clay is fired, the added water disappears at 350° C. and the chemically bound water disappears at between 500°C. and 900° C. At 900° C. there is also a chemical change.

Some of the different types of clay include:
Ordinary modelling clay (1020 °C.), a red clay very suitable for making small objects and figures. It is cheap but is not thoroughly purified.

Throwing clay (1080 °C.) fires white, red, dark brown or black, and is also suitable for modelling small objects.
Clay with fine grog (1100 °C.) fires white, red, dark brown and black. Particularly suitable for modelling but can also be used on the wheel.
Clay with coarse grog (1100 °C.) fires in the same colours as clay with fine grog.
Clay for stoneware (grès) (1180 - 1280 °C.) fires white or grey.
French grès clay (1300 °C.) fires grey.
Suppliers do not always have the same sorts. This is very general survey, but eventually every potter will find a clay to suit him.

3
You have to learn to feel whether the clay is ready for use.

4
If too much water is added, the resulting sludge cannot be used as clay. This is the method for making slip.

5

One of the most effective methods of losing too much water is to pour the clay onto a plaster board and spread it out. The plaster will soak up the water.

6

After a while, depending on the temperature of the air, the clay will be of the required consistency.

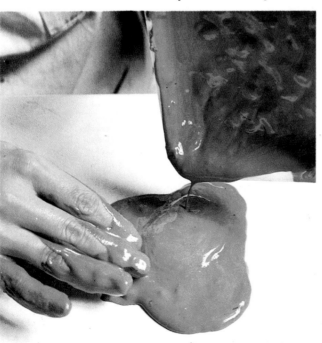

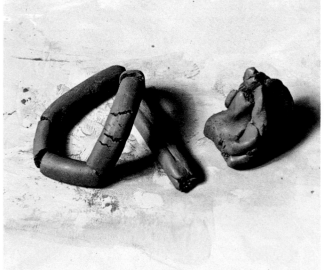

Five stages in biscuit firing
1. At 900° C. a chemical change takes place in the clay.
2. When the temperature rises, the clay shrinks and becomes harder and stronger.
3. This is the vitrifying temperature, which is different for each type of clay.
4. At even higher temperatures the clay loses its shape and the piece will collapse.
5. The melting point has been reached. The clay available in shops shows maximum temperatures. With home-made clay you will have to carry out tests to find out the maximum temperature.

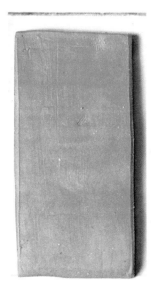

Determining the kneading qualities

To determine whether the clay is suitable for working, roll out a short snake and bend it a few times. If there are any cracks or tears, it is necessary to add water or mix the clay with some other clay with greater plasticity.

1. This clay is impure and unusable.
2. This black firing clay contains manganese and can be folded without cracking.
3. This clay contains iron and will fire red. It could be used if water were added.
4. After adding water the cracks and tears have disappeared.
5. This clay fires to a cream colour. There are some fine cracks so it is possible to add bentonite (maximum 2-3%).

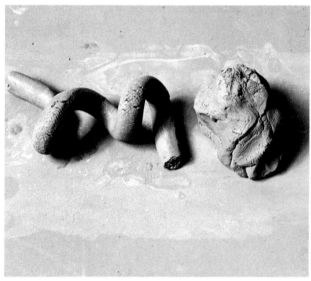

The first pot

It is advisable to use ordinary red modelling clay for your first experiment. This clay is cheap, but it is not thoroughly purified. Sometimes it contains small pebbles, pieces of grit or other impurities.

This causes problems during the firing because the chance of a crack is increased. On the other hand, this clay is easy to work. You must remember that it will take time to learn how to work with clay.

It is not a good idea to start ambitious projects immediately. The firing requires a great deal of energy and should only be done for the best pieces. The following results were obtained by following the step-by-step instructions with the photographs.

1
A lump of clay.

2
Roll out cylindrical lengths of clay by pressing down lightly with the fingers or palms of the hands and rolling from the centre outwards.

3
If you increase the pressure, the coils become longer and thinner. Keep them under plastic to prevent them from drying out.

4
For the bottom of the piece, roll a small ball and press into a circle by pressing from the centre outwards. Place the first coil on the bottom.

5
A cross section of the long part of the coil being pressed into position.

6
Continue until the pot has reached the right height.

7
Stroke down the rounded surface of the coils with the fingers, if possible, the fingertips. In this way the coils are joined together.

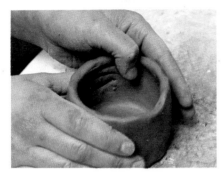

8
Do the same on the inside. The top edge should be smoothed so that it is straight.

9
To make the handle, carefully flatten one of the coils with the tips of the fingers. Cut off two pieces the same length.

10
Slowly bend these pieces into the required shape.

11
Press the top against the pot and join onto the clay on the edge. Press the bottom against the pot, at the same time pressing in the inside of the pot with the index finger to counter this pressure.

12
Make sure the handles are directly opposite each other.

13
Repeat step 4 for the lid. This should be the same size as the bottom. Place a coil on the inside to prevent the lid from slipping. The lid should fit exactly on the pot.

14
Make a handle or a knob for the lid.

15
Use your imagination to decorate this pot.

A simple project

For this design you can use a different sort of clay, possibly a clay that fires white or black. Eventually you will learn from experience what are the various problems and possibilities with different sorts of clay. It is a good idea to make a note of all your experiences in an exercise book, preferably one with a waterproof cover. As rectangular shapes require extremely straight lines, the clay for this exercise is used in slabs rather than coils.

Before using the clay it must be worked to remove any pockets of air (illustrations 2 and 3). If air is trapped in the clay, this will lead to considerable problems during firing. The air expands when it is heated, and this can result in cracks or breaks. To prevent this, all the air must be removed from the clay by 'wedging' it. This process is difficult to photograph but can be described as follows. Using a damp plaster board (a dry one soaks up water from the clay), push and pull on the lump of clay with both hands as though you are rolling it up. You pull the clay towards you with your fingers and then push it away, rather like the movement used in kneading dough when you are baking bread.

When you have repeated this movement a number of times, place the roll which has been formed on its end and start the wedging process all over again.

We do not wish to discourage the beginner, but you can only really guarantee that the clay will be without pockets of air when it has been wedged sixty times, and it is necessary to practise every day for six months to become really proficient at this exercise. When the clay has been wedged, store it in a plastic bag to prevent it from drying out.

The art of doing: Ceramic Techniques

1
On a wooden board, nail down two parallel pieces of wood 7 mm wide. This determines the thickness of the walls of your piece.

2
The pulling and pushing movement used in the wedging.

3
Press out the clay between the two pieces of wood.

4
Roll out the clay with the rolling pin until it is quite smooth.

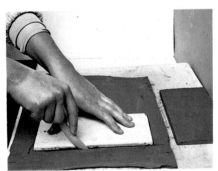

5
Using a rectangular piece of wood or another tool, cut out the six slabs of clay needed for this piece.

6
Lie the slabs next to each other in the required positions. Roughen the edges which are to be joined together by scratching them.

7
Apply some slip along these edges. Slip is clay thinned down with water, which is used as an adhesive.

8
Carefully press the slabs together.

9
Reinforce the joins between the bottom and the sides and between the sides themselves with a thin coil of clay. Carefully smooth these with a modelling tool or with the fingers.

10
When the box is completely shut, leave to dry for a few hours until it is leather hard, and then draw a line with a ruler to show where the lid is to be cut. Cut off the lid absolutely straight with a long darning needle or a special tool for this purpose.

21

11
Place a thin coil of clay along the inside of the lid to prevent the lid from slipping off the box.

12
With a straight piece of wood or a ruler, smooth the outside of the box. In our example a saw is used, and this also makes a pattern.

13
You can add decorative touches with a wooden modelling tool.

The position of the hands

It is a good idea to read this chapter in conjunction with the instructions given with the pictures, and then to have a second look at the pictures. Cross sections of the pots show what the fingers are doing inside them. There is also a description of how to cut off a pot, because it is better to practise this first with a lump of clay. Before cutting off the pot, you first have to clean the wheel around the pot – or in this case, the lump of clay. The clay cutter should be pressed down on the wheel behind the pot, stretched tautly between the fingers of both hands by winding a few times round the fingers.

Turn the wheel once slowly, at the same time pulling the wire towards you. The thumbs should be placed outside the central line of the pot. Make sure that the pattern on the bottom of the pot looks rather like a shell decoration. This is the most attractive pattern and is obtained by turning the wheel just once. As soon as the pot has been removed, pick it up carefully with both hands but without hesitation, and place it on a plaster board or wooden board.

Turn over after a few hours so that the bottom also dries evenly. Turn over larger works regularly.

When the pot is too soft, cut a circle of newspaper slightly larger than the opening of the pot, moisten the newspaper and place on the opening. This keeps the air out so that the pot will retain its shape when it is moved.

1

Widen the opening by pressing the thumbs outwards with the thumbs inside and the fingers on the outside of the pot (cf. step 17 of the following chapter).

2

One thumb pressed against the outside, the other presses on the top edge to prevent it cracking as a result of widening the opening.

3

Press down gently with both hands to check whether the clay is centred.

4

Press with both hands to pull up the walls and make the pot higher (cf. step 19 of the following chapter).

5

Repeat the pulling up process from the bottom upwards, pressing evenly (cf. step 22 of the following chapter).

6

Exert slightly more pressure with the hand inside the pot to obtain a rounded shape.

7

To bend the top edge inwards to outwards, position the hands as indicated in the photograph.

8

To make the pot go in, exert pressure with the hand on the outside of the pot.

9

To make the pot go out, exert pressure with the hand inside the pot.

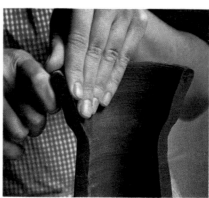

10

Finish off the edge by applying even pressure with the thumb and fingers.

Learning to work the clay on the wheel

As we have discussed the wedging process in detail on p.20, this aspect will only be briefly mentioned in the first three pictures. The clay used on the wheel should not be too hard or too soft, but it is difficult to give a hard and fast rule in this matter. Every potter has his own preference, but for a first attempt it is not advisable to use a very coarse lump of clay.

If the pot or vase is a failure, there is no need to throw away the clay, because it can be used again. It tends to go rather soft after it has been turned on the wheel. If this is the case, the lump should be placed on a dry plaster board for a few hours and turned from time to time. The place where it is in direct contact with the plaster board will dry out first (plaster absorbs water). When the clay is sufficiently dry, it must be wedged again.

There are some types of clay which should never be mixed together. It is best to label the wedged clay, to use plastic covers and to make sure that these are properly sealed; the clay will dry out even if there is only a very small opening.

If the clay is too dry, it does not have to be thrown away. In this case, leave it to dry out completely. Then smash up the dried out clay with the back of an axe. Put all the pieces in a bucket of water. Wait a day and then pour away the excess water and ladle the sediment onto dry plaster board. After another day, turn the clay and leave to dry until it is ready to wedge again.

1

Wedging the clay on a wet plaster board by pressing the clay down.

2

Wedging with the palms of the hands, rolling and pushing away.

3

Wedge the clay, rolling and pushing away.

4

Place a small amount of clay in the centre of the wheel. This will spread out when it is turned.

5

Press down the clay with the tips of the fingers.

6

Continue turning until a large part of the wheel is covered.

7

Then place the lump of clay on the wheel as centrally as possible. Stop the wheel to do this, though when you are sufficiently experienced you will find that it is possible to place the clay on the wheel while it is turning.

8

Turn the wheel. Wet the clay and hands with water from a pail next to the wheel. (In some cases the water container is built into the wheel.)

9

Turn the wheel faster. The clay is centred by pressing the palms of the hands together.

10

The clay assumes a conical shape under the pressure of the hands. Keep on wetting the clay and the hands regularly.

11 With one hand – in this case, the right hand – push down towards the base to make a lower shape. The other hand ensures that the clay continues to remain centred.

12 Press down on the clay with both hands.

13 To prevent the top part from becoming mushroom-shaped, press with one hand while holding the other hand against the side.

14 Check that the clay is still centred by holding the hands around it as shown in the photograph.

15 With the thumbs exert a slight constant pressure to obtain a flat surface. Find the centre of this surface.

16 Press the thumb straight down in the centre to 1 cm from the base. Before putting the thumb in check with a pin while the wheel is not turning.

17 With the thumbs on the inside and the fingers on the outside, widen the opening by pressing the thumbs outwards.

18 Widen the hollow and gently press down towards the base to keep the clay centred.

19 When the opening is large enough pull the clay up, pressing gently with the hand inside the pot and a crooked index finger on the outside. The pressure at the base of the pot should be greater at first and then gradually decrease.

20 Hold the hands as shown in the photograph to keep the opening centred.

21

Keeping the hands in the same position, bend the edge slightly outwards and make a ring. This prevents cracking when the walls are pulled further up.

22

Repeat the pulling up process. Exert an even pressure inside and outside from the bottom upwards.

23

Bend the edge outwards with the index and middle fingers so that the opening is narrower; the other hand supports this movement.

24

Finish off the edge by turning the clay between the thumb and index finger and pressing down against it with the middle finger of the other hand.

Modelling with the hands

Clay is an easy material to model in an almost infinite variety of ways. For hand made figures the clay should be neither too soft nor too dry.

Wedge the clay thoroughly to remove all pockets of air. It is a good idea to use modelling tools because the clay can dry out if it is worked by the hands for a long time, as a result of body heat. For this section we have chosen a plastic bottle as a subject because this lends itself to various interesting possibilities. It is essential to examine any object you are going to copy very carefully. Aesthetic considerations are not the prime concern; the object of the exercise is to acquire some skill in modelling. When the subject is fairly large, as in the case of this bottle, it is a good idea to prick a hole in the bottom to prevent tears and cracks during the firing. For larger holes use an apple corer. You will find some ordinary kitchen utensils very useful for decorating your work. For example, a grater can be used to create a rough surface texture, or an attractive pattern can be obtained by pricking the points of a bunch of meat skewers carefully into the surface of the clay.

As the clay shrinks when it dries, the clay supports – which also shrink – should be regularly checked.

It is not a good idea to use supports made of a different material. If you do, and the supports do not shrink while the model does, parts of the model could break off. If you are making a fairly large model, it is advisable to incorporate some grog in the clay. This is clay which has been fired and is then finely ground, and it comes in carying degrees of fineness. To obtain a fine structure you should use a fine grog.

When you are using grog, first lie some clay on a plaster board, followed by grog, more clay, more grog, and so on. There is a large chance that coarse grog will scratch pieces of plaster from the plaster board. Pieces of plaster in the clay inevitably produce breakages. If it is not possible to finish your model in one go, it should be put away on a wet plaster board covered by a damp cloth and completely enclosed in plastic. Check that the cloth stays damp every day. In summer the clay tends to dry out more quickly, while in winter you must make sure that the clay does not freeze up and become useless as a result.

1
A plastic bottle was chosen as an exercise for modelling the clay.

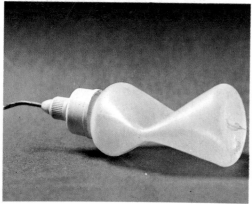

2
Wedging the clay by pulling and pushing it.

3
Divide the lump into two and make the desired shape.

4
Join the two pieces of clay together.

5 Make the right shape by adding bits of clay where necessary.

6 Smooth out any lines or irregularities with a modelling tool.

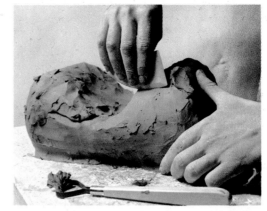

7 Smooth the surface with a modelling tool.

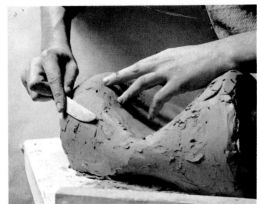

8 Make the bottle top from another piece of clay.

9 Stick the top to the body of the bottle with slip.

10 Finish off the edges with a modelling tool.

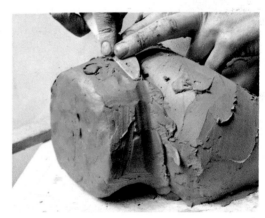

11 Emphasize the transition from the top to the bottom of the bottle.

12 Smooth the top of the bottle top and the other part of the bottle.

13 Remove excess clay with a mirette.

14 Scratch the top of the bottle top and the other part of the bottle.

15 Moisten both surfaces with some slip on a brush.

16 Firmly stick the two parts together.

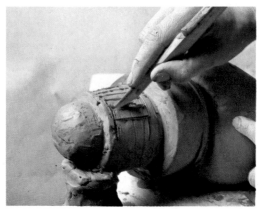

17 Place a clay support under the bottle top to prevent it breaking off. Use the same type of clay for this.

18 Cut grooves in the top and smooth out.

19 Roll a coil for the spout.

20 Cut the coil to the required length.

21 Scratch both parts and join together with slip.

22 Fold an extra strip of clay and bend the spout.

Two models of hand-made vases.

Progressing on the wheel

The next project is a rounded pot with a lid. It is a good idea to copy this pot as exactly as possible. A good potter will know exactly what the end product will look like. To make a strong pot with a good design, it is not advisable to give the pot any shape other than the final shape required while you are turning it. Steps 3 and 4 are the same as steps 5 and 6 on p.26. In photograph 22 some of the centred clay is used for the lid of the pot. This is known as 'throwing off the hump'. This method is generally used when a number of small objects are made with the same shape and size. For a beginner this is the easiest method, though it does mean that the lid is rather heavy.
To prevent breakages during the firing it is advisable to make a hole in the bottom of the pot after it has dried fairly hard. An apple corer is the instrument to use. If necessary, this hole can be elaborated later on. Another method is to place the lid upside down in a suitable low container after it has dried and gone fairly hard, placing this exactly in the centre of the wheel. Attach the wheel to the object with three pieces of wet clay and then attach the object on the wheel with three pieces of clay.
Turning the wheel slowly remove the excess clay with a mirette. The mirette is held still and the clay is peeled off the lid while it is turning.

1

Wedging the clay on a wet plaster board, pressing the clay down.

2

Wedging – the pushing and pulling movements.

3

Spread a piece of clay from the centre outwards by turning the wheel.

4

Keep doing this until a large part of the wheel is covered.

5

Place a lump of clay as centrally as possible on the wheel.

6

Wet the hands and the clay.

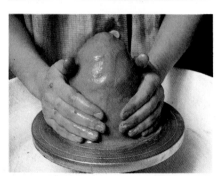

7

Turn the wheel faster. Centre the clay by pressing the palms of the hands together.

8

After the steps described on p.27, press the thumb straight down to 1 cm from the base. See no. 16, p.27.

9

After the steps described on p.27, bend the edges outwards and form the ring.

10

Pull up the pot pressing evenly with both hands.

11

To make the rounded shape pull up the walls from the bottom exerting slightly more pressure with the hand inside the pot.

12

To make the pot go in again increase the pressure of the hand outside.

13

Again exert pressure with the inside hand from the bottom upwards to create a more rounded shape.

14

While the wheel is turning put a needle or sharp object on the edge to remove the excess clay.

15

The upper hand is pushed further out. Do not turn too fast.

16

Finish off the top edge with the little finger, turning the wheel slightly faster.

17

Take off the pot and place on a plaster board. Scratch the surface where the handles are to go.

18

Apply some slip to the scratched area.

19

Attach the handles.

20

Make sure that the handles are directly opposite each other.

21 Take another piece of wedged clay. Wet the clay and hands. Centre the clay.

22 Work up the clay needed for the lid.

23 The top of the lid is formed by a second, more pronounced narrowing.

24 Turn the edge of the lid out with the thumb and index finger.

25 Continue forming the lid between the fingers.

26 Measure the diameter of the opening of the pot with a pair of compasses.

27 On the lid draw a circle with the diameter as the opening.

28 Cut off the excess clay with an awl and finish off the edge.

29 Cut the lid off straight with a clay cutter.

30 Try the lid for size and make a hole using an apple corer when it has dried hard. The lid is rather heavy, and this may result in breakage.

Making a relief model

Again we have chosen an example which incorporates many different technical problems. The relief is built up on a flat plane with pieces of clay, using a knife, modelling spatulas, a mirette, an awl and fine brushes.
The work surface should have two parallel pieces of wood about 2 to 2.5 cm, nailed down. Spread a damp piece of linen on the plank to prevent drying out. If you do not have time to complete the relief at one sitting, it must be covered with plastic. If it is left for quite a while it is a good idea to cover it with a damp cloth under the plastic. Draw the design first, the correct size, on a fairly thin sheet of paper.

1

The tools and
materials needed.

2

Press the clay down
into the plank covered
with a cloth, starting
at the edges.

3

Carefully press down
more clay making sure
there are no pockets of
trapped air.

4

When the surface is
covered, smooth out
the clay with a rolling
pin or a wooden stick.

5

Place the design on the clay and go over the lines with an awl.

6

Remove the paper and check that all the lines are thoroughly pressed through.

7

Cut out the figure with a knife or needle.

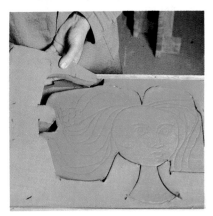

8

Remove excess clay.

9

Now you are ready to start the real modelling.

10

While constanly checking against the example, create differences in depth by removing clay in some places.

11

Mark the places which have been given some depth with a serrated wooden modelling tool.

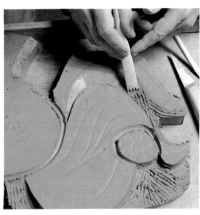

12

Repeat this step wherever you have created relief.

13
Again compare with the example.

14
Add bits of clay where the relief needs extra height.

15
Merge in these pieces of clay with the finger.

16
Finish off the head.

17
Cover the surface of the model with a thin layer of slip or water, using a brush.

18
Leave the slip or water to soak in.

19

To prevent cracks during the firing, divide the figure into pieces.

20

The figure is divided into three pieces.

21

These pieces are carefully turned over.

22

Place the pieces on a folded piece of cloth and indicate which parts should be hollowed out with lines.

23

Remove excess clay with a mirette; the chance that the work will crack during the firing is now reduced.

24

The remaning edges are still quite thick.

25

To ensure that any air pockets which may be trapped in the clay can escape, prick small holes with an awl.

26

This is what the back of the model should look like when it has been hollowed out.

27

When the figure has been fired and is placed on the drawing, you can clearly see how much the clay has shrunk.

Making a cylin- drical pot

It is a good exercise to try and make a cylindrical shape as tall as possible. Drawing up the sides of the vase often proves to be a problem at first. The cylindrical shape provides all sorts of possibilities for other forms and you can experiment with different tops for your vase.

If you wish to make a long neck tapering to a narrow opening, your hands should be held slightly higher than in shown in photograph 18. Holding the middle fingers and thumbs round the place where the neck begins, press gently upwards. Draw up the clay from this place and again press with both hands until the desired shape is achieved. If the opening is too narrow to place a finger of the left hand inside the pot, use a stick, though at first you will find this quite difficult.

If the clay becomes too uneven at the top, it can be removed by holding a needle or sharp awl firmly against the pot at the correct height. This will cut the edge as the wheel is turning. Turn the wheel once and lift the ring of clay that has been cut off out of the way and remove it. It is a good idea to make a drawing of the pot or vase you are making so that you can follow your design more exactly. Only draw the outline profile. At first it is best to draw your design on a piece of card and regularly compare it with the pot you are making.

1
When the clay has been thoroughly wedged, apply a thin layer of clay to the wheel to attach the rest of the clay.

2
Put the clay on the middle of the wheel.

3
Centre the clay by pressing with both hands.

4 Make the clay flat by pressing down on the top.

5 Make an opening in the centre with the thumbs.

6 Press the thumb straight down to within 1 cm of the base.

7 Widen the opening by pressing the thumb outwards. Exert a slight counter pressure with the palms of the hands.

8 Widen the opening with the right hand, protecting the edge with the right thumb.

9 Check that the clay is still centred with both hands.

10
In this way you check the edge.

11
Draw up the sides by exerting pressure with the hands inside and outside the pot.

12
Support the pot with the hand outside the pot while the other hand pinches the clay so that it is drawn up.

13
Do not turn the wheel too fast and continue drawing up the walls as described in the previous chapters.

14
Continue drawing up the clay. The higher you draw up the clay, the more difficult it becomes.

15
When you are drawing up the walls constantly check the edge and keep it smooth with the thumbs or fingers. The edge can crack when the clay is drawn up.

16 Smooth the top so that the edge is even.

17 Check the thickness of the sides from top to bottom.

18 Make the outside wall straight by moving both hands up the side.

19 Press the knuckle of the right index finger inwards and the knuckle of the left index finger outwards slightly higher up.

20 Make a shape for the top of the pot.

21 Cut the vase free with a single movement.

Variations on the cylindrical theme

In the chapter on how to make a cylindrical shape we mentioned the possibility of making variations on this theme. Once you have practised enough so that you no longer have any problems with the cylindrical shape, you will be able to make the vases shown on the following pages without too much difficulty.

In the first three examples it is quite obvious that they are turned, based on this shape; the fourth vase had a very broad base and the rounded shape was made straightaway.

It is advisable to turn the wheel more slowly as the vase gets higher. A slight uncontrolled movement can result in the top of the vase no longer being centred, and the pot will start to go out of true while the clay will become very uneven.

On page 10 you will find a description of the composition of clay which consists of flat particles. When the spaces between these particles are irregular, this can result in cracks or folds which are difficult to remove.

As virtually all the successive steps have been described in the preceding chapters, only the most important are illustrated here.

1

Exert pressure with the palms of the hands, at the same time pressing down in the middle with the thumbs to make the opening.

2

Press the thumbs vertically down.

3

With the knuckle of the right index finger gently press the clay down the inside wall.

4

Draw the cylindrical shape up from the bottom upwards so that the walls become thinner.

5

Continue doing this until the required height is reached.

6

You can create the spherical shape at the top by pressing more firmly from the inside.

7
The knuckle of the middle finger presses the clay inwards while the index finger supports the side. The left hand keeps the vase centred.

8
Make the opening narrower by pressing in and then up with the index finger of the right hand. The middle finger of the left hand is crooked as a support.

9
This movement is repeated until the opening is as narrow as you wish it to be.

10
Correct the bottom half of the vase from the base to the spherical part with a profile, keeping the vase centralised with the left hand.

11
For the second vase the cylindrical shape is also used as a starting point.

12
The rounded shape is created by pressing against the inside wall, while the right hand acts as a counter support.

13

The narrow neck is made by pressing the clay between the thumb and two fingers of the left hand, and at the same time pressing it up. The right index finger supports the vase on the other side.

14

To obtain this saucer-shaped top the opening should be made even narrower with the two thumbs and index finger until the top folds over.

15

Correct any irregularities on the surface with the profile.

16

For the third shape the cylinder is again used as a starting point.

17

To make the vase taper towards the top, the palms of the hands should be placed around it and pressed towards each other and upwards.

18

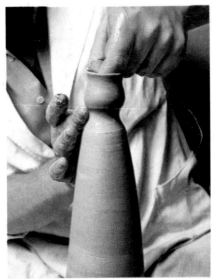

For the bottom of the spherical shape the pressure inside the vase should be greater than the pressure on the outside. When you have reached the middle of this shape the pressure on the outside should be greater than that on the inside.

19

When you are making the edge narrower, press the right middle finger in and up. The left index finger is at the same time slowly drawn up (the fingers taper at the end). If your index finger is too wide, use the left little finger.

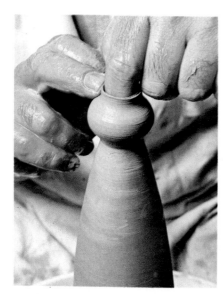

20

The join between the bottom of the vase and the spherical part should be corrected with the thumb and index finger.

21

This vase is made in a spherical shape straightaway, starting with a wide base.

22

Press inwards and up with the right little finger. At the same time the left thumb supports the lip which automatically moves outwards.
The crooked left middle finger ensures that the little finger does not go through the wall.

23

Pull out the edge gently holding the right index and middle finger like a pair of scissors, with the left hand supporting the edge.

24

Repeat this movement until the wall is sufficiently thin. With two fingers above and the thumb and ring finger supporting, make the rounded part of the vase. All the fingers of the left hand support the vase.

Various different vases based on the cylindrical shape.

Ajour technique

To cut out decorative patterns the clay should be leather hard, but not so hard that it will break. If too much clay is removed accidentally it is no longer possible to rectify the mistake. This technique reached a peak in the Chinese Ming period (14th - 16th century) and has been used in Europe since the 17th century.

1

This photograph shows the vase and the tools you will need on a turntable. When you are working on the vase, remove the tools.

2

Begin by indicating the required height of the pattern with a pencil. When you have worked out the pattern, mark the motifs with a pair of compasses and go over this with a pencil.

3

Cut a deeper groove along the lines of the pattern with an awl.

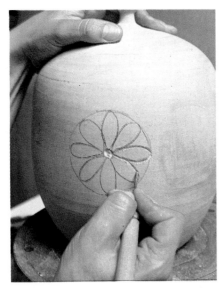

4

Make a hole in the middle of the motif.

5

Remove the clay between the petals of the flower with a larger awl or small knife.

6

Continue removing the clay until the whole pattern is worked open.

7
Make the petals the required shape. Each petal should have a groove down the middle.

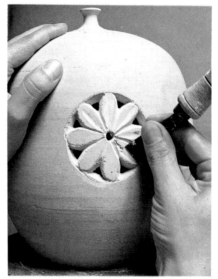

8
Make the three triangles between the rosettes with an awl and remove the clay.

9
The awl should be held at an angle so that the edges slope away.

10
Smooth out and finish off the parts that have been worked open with a damp brush.

11
Go round the whole vase. Finish off the difficult and inaccessible parts with a very fine brush.

12
Leave the vase to dry thoroughly before firing.

13
Another example in
which geometric
figures are cut out.

14
Using a paper cut-out
pattern, scratch the
lines of the motifs.

15
Make the lines deeper
with an awl or needle.

16
Remove the top layer
which makes it easier
to cut into the clay.

17
Carefully cut out the
pieces.

18
Finish off the edges
diagonally.

19
Finish off the edges with sandpaper.

20
Leave to dry thoroughly.

21
In this third example, transfer a motif which has been cut out of paper onto the clay.

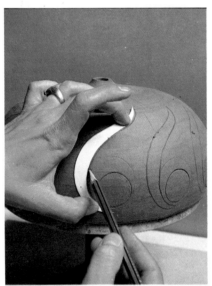

22
Carefully cut out the figures with a knife or needle.

23
Lift out the cut-out shapes.

24
Finish off with a damp brush, then leave the pot to dry, and finally sand down with very fine sandpaper.

Producing different types of pots

The instruments used for producing different sorts of pots will be different for every potter. In the original design you must consider how the work will be executed. If the base or the sides are too thin, it will not be possible to correct this. It is best to leave the clay slightly thicker in places where a pot is narrower; for example, just below the knob of a lid. You cannot turn a bowl which has been made too thick into a smaller elegant bowl later on. The examples in this book are intended as exercises, and to illustrate all the steps clearly some of the objects have deliberately been left too thick.

In illustration 1 the potter puts the finishing touches to a bowl. When the bowl has been cut off the wheel, leave it to go hard. If the clay is too soft, the bowl will change shape when it is turned upside down. Usually a potter will turn a series of pots, vases or bowls on the wheel and then finish them off the next day. This is less time consuming. Photographs 6 and 8 show how a bowl is finished off with a profile on the outside and inside. This is necessary to correct any mistakes or to make a lid fit a top exactly. However, it does make the surface of the bowl very smooth and consequently it no longer looks hand made. Photographs 12 shows a lot of clay being removed; obviously this work had a very thick base. When pots are turned they must be placed exactly in the centre of the wheel and secured with three pieces of soft clay to prevent them moving.

1
The bowl for which the foot has to be turned.

2
The bowl is turned over and held in place with three pieces of clay. Choose an instrument to turn the foot.

3
Smooth the base of the bowl and indicate the outer edge.

4
Scrape out the clay inside the circle with a circular movement so that there is a ring on the base for the bowl to stand on.

5
Finish off the ring on the base.

6
Correct the outside of the bowl with a profile.

7
Finish off the rim of the bowl.

8
Correct the inside with a profile.

9
The bowl is finished.

10
Turning a lid, keep enough clay at the bottom for a handle.

11
Turn the inside edge of the lid. Press in with the middle finger of the right hand while countering this by pressing with the left index finger and middle finger.

12
Cut off the lid and turn over. Take out the clay for the handle.

13
Make the groove under the handle deeper.

14
Round off the handle.

15
Correct any mistakes.

16
Place the lid upside down in the pot, which is placed exactly in the centre of the wheel and secured with three pieces of soft clay. Finish off the edge of the lid so that it fits exactly.

17
Remove the excess clay inside the edge with an awl.

18
Place the lid on the pot and even up with the rest of the pot.

19
In this photograph a bowl is 'thrown from the hump'.

20
The bowl is cut off and left to go slightly hard. It is then turned round, placed in the middle of the wheel and the excess clay is removed.

21
Smooth the bottom.

22
Remove the clay inside the circle to form a ring on the base.

23
For the base, remove the clay from the side.

24 Turn the bowl round and again hold it in place with three pieces of clay. Correct the outside, if necessary supporting the inside with two fingers.

25 Finish off the rim with a knife or the fingers.

26 This is the final product.

27 When you are making a dish, gently press the hands outwards instead of upwards.

28 Smooth the rim thoroughly without pressing down at all.

29 Smooth the dish with a damp sponge while turning the wheel.

30 When the dish is quite hard, turn it upside down and finish off the base to the required diameter.

31 Smooth the base.

32 Remove the clay outside the circle to make a base.

33 If necessary, make corrections from the top to the bottom.

Throwing off the hump

Throwing off the hump is a way of making a large number of small objects one after another without having to start with a new lump of clay every time. A fairly large lump of clay is centred in the normal way. The objects are turned from the top and cut off. As the size of the hump increases towards the bottom, it should be drawn up with both hands after each object is made, until it reaches the required thickness.

This method is particularly suitable, for example, for making a series of small bowls of the same size.

A first it is a good idea to use a profile cut out of wood or perspex as a guide for determining the sides of the bowl.

As the clay is turning past the profile, it becomes this shape.

However, using a profile makes the sides very smooth, which makes the bowls look machine made. The finger prints which are so characteristic of hand made pieces are erased.

The same objection also applies to the use of a profile as seen in photograph 8, p.62 The profile can be in the shape of a rectangle, semi-circle, half oval or spatula. It has sharp edges and is made of a hard wood, aluminium or flexible steel.

The rectangular variety has rounded corners and can be very useful for drawing up the clay into a high side for a pot, instead of using the right index finger.

Once the inside has been drawn up, go back to using your fingers. These tools are very good for correcting mistakes.

A hardwood pair of compasses is an essential tool for making a lid. Photographs 26 and 27 on p.37 clearly show how these are used.

Glazes and their composition

A glaze is a vitreous layer which can be applied to ceramic ware after it has been fired to make the product non-porous, as well as more durable and more beautiful.
Glazes can be roughly divided into:
1. Raw glazes (unfritted glazes).
2. Fritted glazes.
3. Salt glazes. (At 1200° C. salt is sprinkled into a special kiln and the sodium combines with the clay to form a glaze, e.g., in Cologne pots).
4. Ash glazes. (At high temperatures the components, e.g., of wood ash, form a compound with the clay and this compound is a glaze.)
For *raw glazes* the raw materials are ground in a mill or pounded in a pestle and then used in their natural state.

Fritted glazes are glazes of which the raw materials are ground and then melted in the kiln. They are then plunged in cold water when they have reached a very high temperature. Finally they are ground fine and put through a sieve.

There are transparent, semi-transparent and opaque glazes of both types, depending on their composition and suitability at different temperatures. In a good shop selling artists' materials you will be able to buy different types of glaze ready to use in a variety of colours.

You will need some knowledge of chemistry to make your own glazes, and at first it is best to buy them ready made. It is possible to experiment by adding different pigments (colouring oxides). These oxides are added in very small percentages, but they react differently in different glazes depending on the raw materials used.

In general the following oxides react as follows:

Iron oxide (rust), yellowish brown (2 - 10% added);
Manganese oxide, purple, (1 - 3% added);
Cobalt oxide, blue (0.5 - 2% added);
Copper oxide, green (1 - 3% added)'
Nickle oxide, a great variety of colours (up to 3% added);
Tin oxide, white (up to 6% added).

The last of these oxides is extremely expensive, covers completely, and is often used in combination with other oxides. This list is by no means comprehensive, and for further information you should read up on this subject in the technical literature. Before using a glaze it is a good idea to carry out a test, using the same clay as that of the object you have made. Every colour reacts differently on different backgrounds. Stick the test plates on a piece of heavy card and label with a code number; make a note of the proportions you have used in an exercise book. You will need a pair of scales to weight the ingredients. If you are using an expensive oxide use just one spoon for all the small amounts. In this way you will learn to estimate quantities yourself. For larger amounts it is advisable to use a pair of scales like those you would use for weighing letters. A grinding mill is another expensive item, but you can achieve the same results with a good, fairly large pestle and mortar.

Instead of an expensive sieve, you can use an old pair of nylon tights on the side that is not laddered. The tights should be stretched over a bowl. When the glaze has been mixed with water, it is passed through a sieve. Keep the remaining glaze and store in a well-sealed pot.

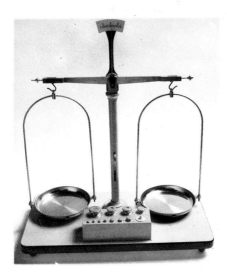

A valuable pair of scales.
This is an essential instrument for the more advanced potter.

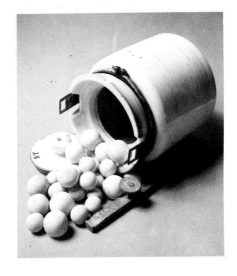

A mill for grinding the glaze. It can be shaken by hand or with an electric motor designed for this purpose.

1

The opening of this vase is made very narrow by pressing the two index fingers together and up.

2

The dry glaze is ground fine in a pestle.

3

Apply the glaze and water mixture to the vase with a brush, thickly in some places, thinly in others.

4

As this glaze tends to drip, place the vase over a draining dish inside the kiln.

5

Where this glaze was applied thickly it has gone blue and crystallized. The crystals can be clearly seen on the photograph below.

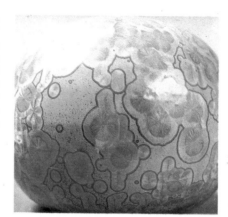

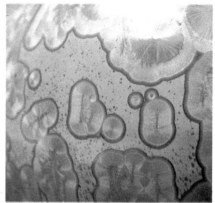

6

Detail of the bottom left part of the vase.

Kilns

Electric kilns are the most popular. If you have access to a chimney, a gas or oil-fired kiln is best. These provide a far wider range of possibilities, for it is possible to fire them with little or no oxygen, producing extremely beautiful colours. If you live in the country and have a large garden, it is even possible to build a kiln yourself from fire bricks. This would be wood-fired. Building a kiln in a built-up area is not recommended, because the smoke that is produced is not appreciated. In these kilns the temperature will rarely rise above 1000° C. They are very suitable for making 'Raku'.

'Raku' is a Japanese pottery technique based on intuition, spontaneity and making the best use of accidents. That is to say that the cracks which result from this method of firing are incorporated in the design. A layman might think that the pot was broken, but a Raku potter is trying to say something with these cracks. The Raku technique originated in Japan in the second half of the 16th century. The objects made in this way were used in the tea ceremony. This ceremony was closely linked with Zen Buddism. The tea masters were true artists who organized the tea ceremonies and contacted potters to make the articles they needed. The teacups were an important part of the ceremony and the most famous tea master, Sen-no-Rikyo commisioned a potter named Chojiro to make a number of teacups. He was the first potter to use the Raku technique. 'Raku' means enjoyment and pleasure, and Rikyo gave this name to Chojiro's successor, who was henceforth known as Jokei Raku. From that time on the pottery technique was known as Raku. Usually the articles are hand made, but they can also be turned on the wheel.

The composition of the clay must be such that it can withstand violent changes in temperature. A sufficient quantity of sand or grog (between 10 - 30%) added to the stoneware produces a porous finish which complies with the requirements of this technique. Unfortunately the glazes used are usually lead glazes which are extremely poisonous. It is best to use a factory glaze which incorporates lead. This glaze is fired beforehand so that it is less dangerous to use. When the article has been biscuit fired in an electric kiln, the outside kiln should be heated to at least 1000° C. This will take a few hours. The now glazed article is placed inside the red hot kiln on a triangle, using a special long pair of pliers. The kiln is shut and after about twenty minutes (depending on the glaze) the article is removed with the pliers and placed inside a box of straw, ferns or grass on which a lid is immediately placed. The straw or grass produces a design on the surface of the glaze. It is also possible to submerge the article immediately in a large tub of water. Obviously the pot itself and the glaze should be able to withstand this rather rough treatment. Before buying a kiln you should find out about the various possibilities. If you choose an electrical kiln it is important to know how many kilowatts you can go to. You will need a three phase electrical plug and a separate lead from the electric meter. There are kilns which can be plugged directlyinto the lighting circuit, but in this case you must make sure that not too many other electrical appliances are used at the same time as the klin. There must be a good chimney available if you opt for a gas or oil-fired kiln.

The temperature of the klin

The firing process is very important, and the temperature must be constantly checked. This can be done simply by looking or with a thermocouple or seger cones. You need a lot of experience to be able to estimate the temperature by looking at the kiln, and a difference of 20-30° C. can be harmful for some glazes.

The colours inside the kiln indicate the following temperatures: red, 700° C.; dark red, 950° C.; orange red, 1100° C.; pale red: 1300° C.; white hot, 1400° C. A thermocouple is an instrument in which the ends of two wires of different materials are welded together. The point at which they are welded is insulated by a porcelain tube which is put in the kiln through a hole in the side. The difference in potential voltage arising in the thermocouple depends on the temperature. The thermocouple is joined to the pyrometer with to wires, and the temperature can be read off the pyrometer.

Cones used to to indicate the temperature are placed in lumps of clay so that they are visible through a peep hole in the kiln. The numbers of the cones indicate the different temperatures. As soon as a cone bends over, the temperature shown on this cone has been reached. The problem with these cones is to make sure that they are visible inside the oven. Opening the lid or door of the kiln leads to a great loss of energy, and a peep hole often only provides a limited view. A thermocouple with a pyrometer is admittedly expensieve, but it is also a more precise way of measuring the temperature. If you are using cones, these must be placed in various places in the kiln because the temperature varies not only in the top and bottom of the kiln but also in the middle and in the corners.

Firing the kiln

When an article is ready for firing it must first be thoroughly dried out before being fired. The first firing (biscuit firing) should be done slowly.

The temperature of the biscuit firing is around 1000° C., though it depends on the glaze that is used. In some cases it is better to fire the biscuit 100° C. higher than the glaze needs. The critical temperature is between 600° C. and 900° C. At this temperature the structure of the clay changes.

If the clay contains pockets of air or impurities there is an increased risk of cracks or breakages. The air pockets expand in the heat, the impurities burn in the shard, and gases attempt to escape. Usually you think of 'shard' as the broken pieces of a pot, but for a potter the shard also means the composition of the wall of a pot or vase. After the first firing (biscuit) the article should be allowed to cool slowly. The lid or door of the kiln should not be opened.

The critical point during the cooling process also lies between 600 and 900° C. Unglazed objects can be stacked on top of one another or placed next to each other, as long as the air inside the articles can escape.
Place the heaviest pieces at the bottom. The glaze firing is different in that heat increases fairly rapidly to

600° C. and then slowly to the quartz inversion (firing) temperature. For every glaze this is determined indepently. When the firing temperature is reached this should be maintained for 1 - 1^1/$_2$ hours, depending on the type of glaze used, so that all the gases can escape.

The cooling process of the glaze from the maximum temperature to 600° C. can take place relatively quickly because the glaze is still liquid at this stage. The lid or door of the kiln should only be opened a fraction of an inch if the shard can withstand it.
From 600° C. the kiln should be cooled down very slowly,

more slowly than heating up, because the vitreous layer and the shard should shrink together. Large articles should always be fired more slowly, also during the biscuit firing. Some experience is needed to stoke a kiln, and at first it is advisable to make a note of all the temperatures to enable you to arrive at the correct method.

Errors in glazing

Apart from the elements of which the glaze is composed, there are other factors which play a part in firing the glaze. The same glaze can produce different results even if the ingredients have been mixed in exactly the same way, for example, when:

1. a different clay is used;
2. different water is used (tap water or rain water);
3. there are new raw materials which might be slightly different;
4. the glaze is applied thickly or thinly.

You may discover all sorts of imperfections after your work has been fired. In this chapter some of these are discussed and ideas are put forward about how to avoid them. Sometimes it is possible to correct these mistakes in the glaze, but this requires a thorough knowledge of the preparation of glazes. It is not possible to describe these procedures within the scope of this book. In addition, the climate in the kiln plays an important part. This includes the amount of oxygen or the lack of oxygen in the kiln during firing. Electric kilns usually fire with a lot of oxygen, while gas, oil or wood fired kilns have very little oxygen. For some glazes such as ash glazes it is best to have an oxygen poor climate. This can be achieved by stoking with charcoal. Charcoal burns up oxygen in the surrounding area. The oxygen in the glaze is also used up. This changes the chemical compound of the pigment (e.g., Fe_2O_3, rust, turns to Fe, pure iron), and very special colours such as a soft Chinese green, a blue celadon or the red sang-de-boeuf are produced. This method of firing is called reduction firing. In a simple electric kiln reduction is damaging for the elements. Wood, gas and oil-fired klins are suitable for reduction firing. The usual method of firing a glaze is known as oxidised firing. This book is based on glazes which can be bought in powder form. Many catalogues containing the different types of glaze use the therms 'oxidation' and 'reduction'. A beginner would be well advised to start by using glazes which are fired through oxidation. If the catalogue does not state otherwise, the glaze will be oxidative. Some glazes can be fired by either method. Any article to be glazed must be completely free of dust and grease or the glaze will not adhere to the pot. When you pick up your work take care that you do not leave greasy fingerprints.

Place the vase on a triangle to prevent it from sticking to the floor of the oven; if the glaze you are using tends to drip, place the vase over an earthenware dish so that the glaze can drip into it.

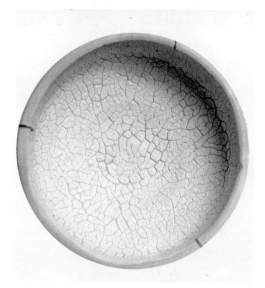

1
These patches are caused by applying the glaze too thickly, dirt underneath the glaze or cracking during the drying process. Another cause might be the fact that the clay and the glaze are not compatible. The way to prevent this is to apply the glaze more thinly and to make sure that the clay base is clean. In some cases the problem can be solved by increasing the temperature by 20 or 30° C.

2
The glaze will come away when it is under great tension and there is too much difference between the rate at which the clay and the glaze shrink. When you are buying the clay and the glaze remember that they should be compatible.

3
The glaze can flake off in a number of places if there are coarse grains of salt or plaster impurities in the clay.

4
Craters and bubbles can form it the glaze is fired at temperatures which are too high and is then cooled down too rapidly. At very high temperatures the glaze will start to bubble. The temperature should be raised slowly to the maturing temperature and then kept constant for at least 45 minutes.

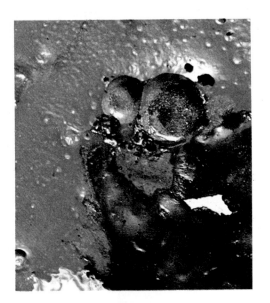

5
If the glaze starts to wrinkle, this means that it has not been applied properly. This can be prevented by spraying the glaze on. Hold the spray at a distance from the article.

6
This glaze has been fired too hot and should be fired at a lower temperature.

Applying the glaze

The example we have chosen is the relief made in an earlier chapter. In the example a foundation glaze was used with coloured oxides (pigments) to create contrasts. The same effect can also be achieved by applying different coloured glazes one over the other, not too thickly. These glazes should have the same composition or have the same characteristics and be compatible with regard to temperature. In general it is better to design a figure which will not require too many colours. The glaze should have a supporting effect on the figure. In this example the glaze is applied like the paint on a painting, but this is not really a ceramic technique. Depending on the figure there are various different ways of applying the glaze: with a brush, turning on the wheel as in photograph 4, or smoothing over the surface.

75

Submerging
This requires a great deal of glaze, usually a bucketful. The article should be completely submerged with a turning movement.
Pouring Usually the glaze should be rinsed round the inside of the article first. Then it can be turned upside down and placed on two pieces of wood over a large bowl. The glaze is poured from a jug over the article as it is turned on a turntable. Remove any large drips with a knife.
Sprinkling. Dip a hard brush in the glaze, and aiming it at the article to be glazed, grate it with a stick.
Spraying. Attach a paint sprayer filled with glaze to the nozzle of a vacuum cleaner and place this on the side that is blowing. It is essential that the sucking action is good, and to protect the mouth and nose, as well as to wear special clothes and cover the hair.

All these different methods require a particular thickness of the glaze, i.e., different amounts of water are added, depending on the way in which the glaze is applied. Before using the glaze it should be sieved while it is wet.
In this way it cannot separate. The special sieves for this are rather expensive, but an old nylon stocking stretched over a fairly shallow dish works just as well. Even glazes bought ready to use should be sieved bacause they will go lumpy if they stand around too long. All traces of dust or grease should be removed from the article, otherwise the glaze will not adhere. The articles are placed in the kiln on fireclay supports. These should be covered with a mixture of equal parts of kaolin and quartz mixed with water, to protect against possible dripping of the glaze. The plates can be stacked using other supports of different sizes which can be bought for this purpose. To prevent the articles being joined together, the glazed articles should be placed quite separately on triangles or other supports.

1
Assemble all the ingredients on a clean work surface.

2
Rub the glaze fine with water in mortar. Put it through a sieve and return it to the mortar.

3
To prevent excessive absorption of the glaze, you can brush the article all over with water.

4
Apply the glaze evenly.

5
Brush all the parts of the figure with the foundation glaze.

6
Leave this to dry.

7
Clean the bottom of the article, holding it carefully but without hesitating.

8
Mix the pigment (coloured oxide) on a glass plate or in a small mortar with the foundation glaze or a melting agent.

9
Add water until the mixture can easily be applied with a brush.

10
Apply this colour where needed, using a brush.

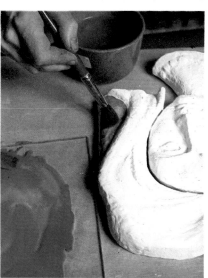

11
Prepare the next colour in the same way.

12
Apply this colour with a brush.

13
Leave it to dry.

14
Put the kiln plates ready.

15
In a mortar mix equal parts of kaolin and quartz with water.

16
Add enough water until the mixture can be brushed on.

17
Rub out all the lumps.

18
Brush this mixture over the kiln plates with a paintbrush.

19
Leave the plates to dry.

20
Stack the plates using props.

21
Place triangles on the plates to prevent the article from sticking.

22
Carefully place the article on these. These photographs were taken *outside* the kiln, but in reality they obviously took place inside the kiln.

Old decoration technique

The tile shown here is an example of an old technique known as 'cloisonné'. The thicker lines should be functional within the design. These lines can be made with thin coils of clay but in some cases it is easier to use a plastic (icing sugar) icer filled with thick slip of the same type of clay. When it has gone hard this material can be finished off very easily. The design is drawn on a piece of paper and then transferred onto the tile. The tile is made in the same way as the parts of the box on page 21; it should be dried between two plaster boards to prevent it warping.

1 The clay coils – if possible keep these in a damp cloth as they dry out rather quickly – tile, brush, water, spatula.

2 Clearly mark the lines of the design by pressing on the paper with the point of a pencil.

3 Brush the slip on the lines with a pencil.

4 Stick down the clay coils.

5 Press down neatly with a spatula. For the rounded corners use the point of the spatula, for the longer bits use the flat side.

6 Finish off the edges.

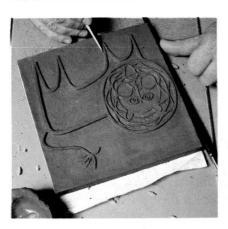

7 The tile can be fired when it has dried out.

8 Get everything ready for applying the glaze.

9 Spread water all over the tile with a wet brush so that the glaze will not be absorbed too much.

10 Mix the glaze with water on a glass plate.

11 With a spatula apply the glaze *inside* the lines.

12 Leave the lines unglazed and if necessary, clean with a damp cloth.

13 Fill in the small planes with a very fine brush.

14 Apply the glaze for the background with a thicker brush.

15 Place the tile in the oven. When it has been fired, you will see its 'true' colours.

Instead of using coils of clay it is also possible to spray on the lines with a plastic icing sugar icer filled with a liquid engobe mixture. Engobe is made from the same clay that was used for the article; this is ground with an oxide (pigment) and if necessary, a melting agent is added.

1

The design is transferred to the clay. It is also possible to scratch it straight onto the clay if you feel confident about drawing it.

2
Fill a rubber balloon or the top of a cream icer with engobe mixture.

3
Spread the engobe evenly over the scratched lines.

4
Leave the tile to dry and then fire it in the kiln.

5
Get everything ready to glaze the tile.

6
Brush water onto the parts of the tile that are to be glazed and rub the glaze fine.

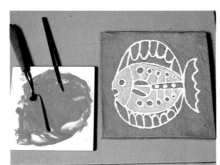

7
With a brush, apply the glaze inside the lines.

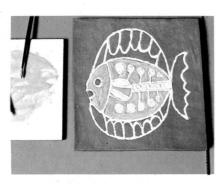

8
Apply each colour separately.

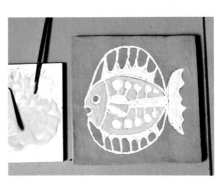

9
Check that the lines of engobe are clean before applying a new colour.

10
Use a thicker glaze for the outer part of the fins.

11
Leave the tile to dry and fire in the kiln. The background remains unglazed.

Decorating with underglaze colour

Underglaze colour can be bought in specialist shops, and like the glaze itself it is mixed with water. It should not be too thick or there will be bare patches in the paint and glaze after the glaze firing.

Photograph 1 shows a bowl on a turntable. A *turntable* is a small, movable disc with can be turned by hand. It is essential for glazing. When you are decorating it is better to have a wheel so that you have both hands free. You will need to support the hand that is decorating with the other hand to prevent it slipping. It is advisable to mark the main features of the decoration with a pencil in advance as it is not possible to correct any mistakes once the underglaze colour has been applied. A transparent layer of glaze is used over the underglaze colour.

When choosing the colours of the paint remember that the natural colour of the clay will appear in those places which have not been decorated. If a spray is used for glazing the article, as in this example, you must wear a mask.

1 The bowl is placed on the turntable. The turntable is a small movable disc which is turned by hand. It is an essential piece of equipment for glazing.

2 Place the bowl in the middle of the turntable or wheel. Slowly turn the wheel while keeping the brush in one place. Apply all the circles in this way in the chosen colours.

3 Apply the star shape in the bottom of the bowl using a thicker brush, painting from the centre outwards to the points.

4 When you are painting the star shape the left hand is used as a support to prevent slipping.

5 Hold the bowl in one hand, supporting the side. With a fine brush, paint in the lines. Turn the bowl through 90° and continue decorating.

6
Put in the dots in the same way.

7
Position the bowl in the middle of the wheel and slowly turn the wheel, applying the chosen colour to the rim.

8
In the same way paint the stripes on the outside of the bowl.

9
Leave the underglaze colour to dry for a while.

10
Add as much frit as necessary to some water in the mortar and rub free.

11
Sieve the prepared frit.

12
Wear a protective mask over the mouth and nose when you are spraying on the frit.

Decorating with overglaze enamel

Overglaze is a glaze which is used to paint or decorate objects which have already been glazed. In order to prevent dripping on a shiny surface this sort of glaze is not mixed with water but with a special medium.

It is easier to use this sort of glaze than underglaze. If mistakes are made in applying it, it is easy to remove from the smooth surface. In addition to the usual colours, it is also possible to buy a shiny or matt gold and silver. These should never be fired at high temperatures because they will turn black. Unlike ordinary glazes, overglazes do not usually change colour when they are fired. Before applying the glaze, remove all traces of grease and dirt from the article. Fire at a fairly low temperature: between 650-700°C. (third firing).

1
Paint the circles on the vase by placing it on a manually operated turntable and keeping the brush still in one place.

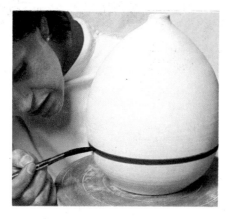

2
Paint on each arch with a single stroke of the brush, making sure that there is enough paint on the brush each time.

3
After doing the first row of arches, start on the second row.

4
As the brush moves higher up the vase, change the angle. For a steady hand, support your painting arm with the other hand.

5
Use a slightly thicker brush for the leaves, starting each motif from the bottom and working upwards. Do not go over the brush strokes a second time.

6
Again support the forearm to prevent the paintbrush from slipping.

7
At the base of the vase the leaf motif is applied horizontally.

8
The red colour that appears in the kiln at 700° C. When the door was opened, the temperature dropped at the front of the kiln, so that the decoration was clearly visible.

Making tools

The tools needed for pottery or clay modelling can be bought at any shop selling artists' materials relatively cheaply. The advantage of home-made tools is that they can be adapted to suit individual needs. You will not need anything apart from an ordinary electric drill, sandpaper and a pair of pliers.

The drill should be firmly secured to the bench or in a special vice so that it cannot move. Fit a (coarse) whetting stone or whetting disc in the drill chuck. To make modelling spatulas it is best to use palm wood. This is a slightly oily wood which prevents the clay from sticking to it.

To make a mirette, use copper or stainless steel wire, as iron wire will soon go rusty. The clay cutter which is used for cutting the articles from the turntable is simple to make. Attach two wooden rods to either side of a length of twisted stainless steel wire. The length of the wire varies according to the size of the articles.

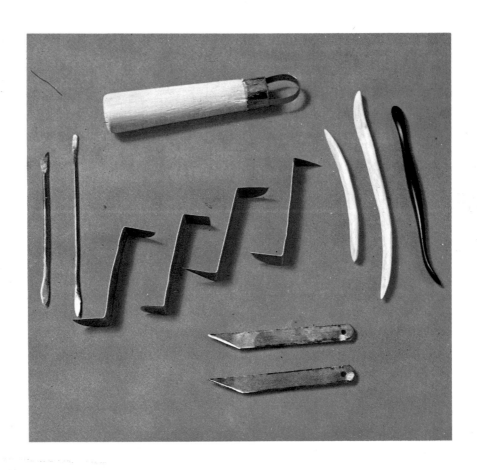

1

For flat metal tools you will need a pair of pliers and some strips of zinc: fit the whetstone on the drill. Wear safety goggles to protect the eyes.

2

Grind the corner until the required shape is obtained.

3

Hold the metal at an angle against the whetstone to grind the edges.

4

For a curved tool bend the metal at right angles with the pliers.

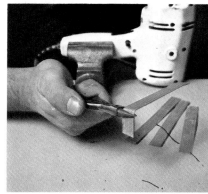

5

Bend in the opposite direction on the other side.

6

Then shape the ends using the whetstone. One end is straight, the other rounded.

7

Another tool can be made with small metal rods.

8

Flatten the end of the rod by hitting it with a hammer on a bar of metal.

9
Tidy up the edge of the flat end.

10
To make the modelling sticks put the sanding disc on the drill.

11
Put the piece of wood over the edges of the disc.

12
Shape the stick to the shape you require by pulling over the disc when it is turning.

13
Shape the spatulas at the ends.

14
Sand thoroughly after sharpening.

15
The stick should be held at an angle in the middle of the disc if you need a flat spatula.

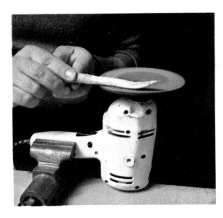

16
Continue letting the disc rotate to finish off the middle of the stick.

17

Finish off one end in a rounded shape at one end, and pointed at the other.

18

Finish off with sandpaper.

The beginner will need the following tools when he takes up pottery:

1. Wheel (electric or kick wheel)
2. Kiln, shelves and a pyrometer
3. Various different triangles
4. Scales
5. Plaster boards
6. Modelling tools and brushes
7. Mortar and pestle (not too small)
8. Sieve or nylon tights and a shallow bowl
9. A fair number of well sealed pots or jars
10. A real sponge
11. A roll of plastic
12. Tables and exercise books with waterproof covers
13. Disposable masks, available from shops selling medical equipment
14. A small, manually operated turntable (you can use an old record player for this)

Another important requirement is plenty of space where you experiment. Finally, remember that if you throw clay down the sink or the washbasin, this can lead to blocked drains. If you don't want a huge plumber's bill, either fit a trap under the sink or rinse the clay in a bucket.

After a while the clay will sink to the bottom. Then the water can be poured away and what remains can be wrapped in newspaper and throuwn in the dustbin if it cannot be used. Before washing your hands, also rinse them in the bucket.